"Morning Blessing"

Margaret Tarrant's
Christmas Garland

Edited by
Marian Russell Heath

DOVER PUBLICATIONS, INC.
Mineola, New York

Bibliographical Note

This Dover edition, first published in 2011, is an unabridged republication of the work originally published by Hale, Cushman & Flint, Boston, in 1942.

Library of Congress Cataloging-in-Publication Data

Margaret Tarrant's Christmas garland.
    A Christmas garland / illustrated by Margaret Tarrant ; edited by Marian Russell Heath.
       p. cm.
    Originally published: Margaret Tarrant's Christmas garland. Boston : Hale, Cushman & Flint, 1942.
    ISBN-13: 978-0-486-48091-6
    ISBN-10: 0-486-48091-7
     1. Tarrant, Margaret, 1888–1959, ill. II. Heath, Marian Russell. III. Title.

PN6071.C6M32 2011
808.8'0334—dc22

                                    2011013660

Manufactured in the United States by Courier Corporation
48091701
www.doverpublications.com

TABLE OF CONTENTS

LIST OF ILLUSTRATIONS

The Christmas Story
According to
Saint Luke

And it came to pass in those days that there went out a decree from Caesar Augustus that all the world should be taxed. And all went to be taxed, every one into his own city. And Joseph also went up from Galilee, out of the city of Nazareth, into Judea, unto the city of David, which is called Bethlehem (because he was of the house and lineage of David), to be taxed with Mary his espoused wife, being great with child .

And so it was, that, while they were there, the days were accomplished that she should be delivered. And she brought forth her firstborn son, and wrapped him in swaddling clothes and laid him in a manger; because there was no room for them in the inn.

And there were in the same country shepherds abiding in the fields, keeping watch over their flocks by night.

And, lo, the angel of the Lord came upon them, and the glory of the Lord shone round about them; and they were sore afraid .

And the angel said unto them, Fear not; for behold, I bring you good tidings of great joy, which shall be to all people. For unto you is born this day in the city of David a Saviour, which is Christ the Lord. And this shall be a sign unto you; Ye shall find the babe wrapped in swaddling clothes, lying in a manger. And suddenly there was with the angel a multitude of heavenly host praising God, and saying, Glory to God in the highest, and on earth peace, good will toward men.

I SALUTE YOU

I am your friend, and my love for you goes deep. There is nothing I can give you which you have not; but there is much, very much, that, while I cannot give it you can take. No heaven can come to us unless our hearts find rest in it today. Take Heaven! No peace lies in the future which is not hidden in this present little instant. Take Peace! The gloom of the world is but a shadow. Behind it yet within our reach, is Joy. There is radiance and glory in the darkness, could we but see; and to See, we

have only to Look.   I   beseech you to
Look.

Life is so generous a giver, but we,
judging its gifts by their
covering, cast them away as ugly
or heavy or hard. Remove the
covering and you will find beneath it
a living splendour, woven of Love,
by Wisdom, with Power.
Welcome it, grasp it, and you touch
the Angel's hand that brings it to
you. Everything we call a trial,
a sorrow, or a duty; believe me, that
Angel's hand is there; the Gift is
there, and the wonder of an overshad-
owing Presence. Our joys, too; be
not content with them as joys. They,

too, conceal diviner Gifts. ▧▨▧▨▧

Life is so full of Meaning and
Purpose, so full of Beauty —
beneath its covering — that you will
find earth but cloaks your Heaven.
Courage then, to claim it; that is all!
But Courage you have: and the ▧▨▧
knowledge that we are pilgrims together,
wending through unknown country ▧▨
Home.
And so, at this time, I greet you:
not quite as the world sends ▧▨▧
greetings, but with profound esteem,
and with the Prayer that for you,
now and forever, the Day breaks,
and the shadows flee away. ▧▨▧▨▧

A Letter Written by
Fra Giovanni ∼ A.D. 1513

REAL CHRISTMAS

Angelo Patri

OUT in a western town where the old mission spirit still lives, the people celebrate Christmas by going to church. On Christmas Eve the altar is dressed with candles and close by, the scene of the Nativity is laid reverently. The Holy Child lies in the manger, His Mother kneeling on one side, His Father on the other. At His feet stand the Three Wise Men bringing gifts. The animals kneel in their stalls, all but the little donkey who peers down into the face of the sleeping Child. A group of shepherds listen to the angel choir and a bright star shines down over all. It is all very sacred in feeling, and very lovely.

Early Christmas morning, before anyone else would be likely to be out, the good priest went to his church to see that all was as it should be for the first service. What was his horror to discover the manger empty and the Christ Child gone. After an unbelieving glance about the place, he rushed out into the street to give the alarm.

The street was empty save for a tiny little boy who pulled a little red wagon behind him. He paced slowly, solemnly toward the church and the good Father was almost on top of him before he noticed him. Imagine his amazement when he saw the missing Christ Child, carefully wrapped in a scarlet sweater, lying in the little wagon.

"What, what's this? How—" But all dread and anger fled from the good man's heart as he looked into the innocent face before

him. He saw that whatever had been done was done for goodness'
sake.

"Tell me why you did this, my son."

"Because, Father, I prayed for a red wagon for Christmas and I
promised that if I got it, I would give the Little Lord Jesus the first
ride. So I did. Now I'm going to take Him back to His Mother and
say a prayer of thanks."

"We will go together," said the priest and, hand in hand, the
old, old man and the very small boy went into the church carrying
the Holy Child.

BABUSHKA

A RUSSIAN LEGEND

Edith M. Thomas

*B*ABUSHKA sits before the fire
   Upon a winter's night;
The driving winds heap up the snow,
   Her hut is snug and tight;
The howling winds, — they only make
   Babushka's fire more bright!

She hears a knocking at the door:
   So late — who can it be?
She hastes to lift the wooden latch,
   No thought of fear has she;
The wind-blown candle in her hand
   Shines out on strangers three.

Their beards are white with age, and snow
   That in the darkness flies;
Their floating locks are long and white,
   But kindly are their eyes
That sparkle underneath their brows,
   Like stars in frosty skies.

"Babushka, we have come from far,
   We tarry but to say,

A little Prince is born this night,
    Who all the world shall sway.
Come join the search, go with us,
    We go our gifts to pay."

Babushka shivers at the door;
    "I would I might behold
The little Prince who shall be King
    But ah! the night is cold,
The wind so fierce, the snow so deep,
    And I, good sirs, am old."

The strangers three, no word they speak,
    But fade in snowy space!
Babushka sits before her fire,
    And dreams, with wistful face:
"I would that I had questioned them,
    So I the way might trace!"

"When morning comes with blessed light,
    I'll early be awake:
My staff in hand I'll go, — perchance,
    Those strangers I'll o'ertake;
And, for the Child some little toys
    I'll carry, for His sake."

The morning came, and staff in hand,
    She wandered in the snow,
She asked the way of all she met,
    But none the way could show.

"Babushka"

"It must be farther yet," she sighed:
    "Then farther will I go."

And still, 'tis said, on Christmas Eve,
    When high the drifts are piled,
With staff, with basket on her arm,
    Babushka seeks the Child:
At every door her face is seen, —
    Her wistful face and mild!

Her gifts at every door she leaves:
    She bends and murmurs low,
Above each little face half-hid
    By pillows white as snow:
"And is He here?" Then, softly sighs,
    "Nay, farther must I go!"

THE CRÈCHE

Alice Gregg

COME, hang the greens and plant the Tree,
    And light the Christmas candles;
Your carols sing of Wise Men Three, —
    Of shepherds in their sandals.

Go, get you straw and get you wood
    And build again the stable,
For you will find it very good
    Who dress in silk and sable.

Go, build again the wooden bed,
    The cattle standing round it,
The straw to pillow His sweet head,
    The Shepherds to surround it.

Then kneel beside the manger bed,
    And feel the loving awe
That takes all simple hearted folk
    Who kneel upon the straw.

"The Crèche"

LITTLE LAMB, WHO MADE THEE?

William Blake

LITTLE lamb, who made thee?
  Dost thou know who made thee,
Gave thee life, and bid thee feed
By the stream and o'er the mead;
Gave thee clothing of delight,
Softest clothing, woolly, bright;
Gave thee such a tender voice,
Making all the vales rejoice?
      Little lamb, who made thee?
      Dost thou know who made thee?
      Little lamb, I'll tell thee;
      Little lamb, I'll tell thee;
He is called by thy name,
For He calls Himself a Lamb.
He is meek, and He is mild,
He became a little child,
I a child, and thou a lamb,
We are called by His name.
      Little lamb, God bless thee!
      Little lamb, God bless thee!

A LITTLE CHILD

Author Unknown

A LITTLE Child,
   A shining star.
A stable rude,
   The door ajar.

Yet in that place,
   So crude, forlorn,
The Hope of all
   The world was born.

O THE MORN

An Early Carol

O THE Morn, the merry merry morn,
   The morn of Christmas-Day,
When God, the Son of God, was born
   Of Mary, maiden ay!

Sweet the Song, the happy happy song,
   Precented at His birth,
And caught up by the heav'nly throng,
   "Good-will, and Peace on Earth!"

To the Town, the tiny tiny town,
   The town of Bethlem, ran
Some simple shepherds, o'er the down,
   To view Him, God and Man.

There within a cattle cattle shed,
   They find and worship Him,
Who rideth, in His realm o'erhead,
   Upon the Cherubim.

So, my Boys, my bonny bonny boys,
   To Bethlem off be we
But, pray you, shun whate'er annoys
   The Babe on Mary's knee.

LOVE AMONGST THE SNOWS

Author Unknown

*L*OVE awoke one winter's night
. And wander'd through the snowbound land,
And calling to the beasts and birds
Bid them his message understand.

And from the forest all wild things
That crept or flew obeyed love's call,
And learned from him the golden words
Of brotherhood for one and all.

"Love Amongst the Snows"

THE STORY OF THE FIELD OF ANGELS

Florence Morse Kingsley

IN the deep valley below Bethlehem an undulating meadow stretches east and west, its grass starred thick with blossoms in the days after the autumn rains. The villagers call it the Field of Angels, though to some it is known as the Place of the Star. In the days of the Caesars the turrets of Migdol Edar, the shepherds' watch tower, still looked down upon the place, though shepherds had long ceased to watch their flocks there by night.

Six miles to the north, behind the scarred shoulders of the ravaged hills, lay shamed and desolate Jerusalem. There was no longer a temple therein whither the tribes of Israel could go up to praise and magnify the name of Jehovah. Of all that great and glorious Zion there remained only a place for wailing by a ruined wall.

But flowers bloomed again in the red tracks of the Roman armies, and again there were little children to whom the horrors of that time of death were only as a tale that is told between waking and sleeping. When the sun shines in unclouded heavens, and myriads of flowers wave in the sweet wind, and the lark floods his acres of sky with down-dropping melody, what young thing will lament ruined temples or yet vanished cities, be they never so glorious? And so, the children were plucking the first flowers in the Field of Angels with shouts and laughter.

In the dwarfed shadow of Migdol Edar sat an old man who talked with himself in the midst of his great silver beard, his blue eyes shining like twinkling pools amid the frosty sedge of a winter's morning. "The young things crop the blossoms like lambs," he muttered, and stretched his withered hand to gather a tuft of the white, starlike flowers. Then he smiled to see a troop of little ones running toward him fearless as the lambs to which he had likened them.

First came a tall girl of ten, her clear olive cheek shaded by a tangle of curls; she held a flower-crowned baby in each hand. Behind her lagged three or four smaller girls and half a score of boys, shyer and more suspicious than their sisters.

"Good sir, wilt thou gather flowers in the Angel Field?" demanded the tall girl fixing bright, questioning eyes upon the stranger.

"Thou hast said truth, maiden," answered the old man.

"I have come from over seas to gather them. And I will also tell thee one thing. Seest thou how many blossoms grow in this low valley? There grows a shining thought for every flower; these also would I gather."

The girl shook her head. "We have found no shining thoughts in this field, honorable stranger," she said. "Here are star flowers, and blue lilies of Israel, and anemones purple and scarlet. There are no flowers like those of the Angel Field. But I would that we might see the shining things which thou hast gathered."

"Sit ye down upon the grass, every child of you," cried the old man, his blue eyes beaming with delight, "and I will show you my shining thoughts, for in truth they are fairer than the flowers which perish in the plucking. See, child, the blue lilies of Israel how they droop and wither, and the star flowers drop their petals like early snow; but I will show you that which can never perish. Look you, children, I was no taller than yon little lad — he with the scarlet tunic; and I wandered with the shepherds in this field — which in those days was known only as the valley of the flocks —

gathering flowers and minding the paschal lambs. They strayed not far from their mothers. Great Jerusalem was in its latter glory, and a marvelous bright star shone in the heavens. Wise men there were who declared that the star heralded the birth of Israel's deliverer, He who should be King of kings and Lord even of the Romans. The shepherds talked of these things in the night watches, and I, folded in my father's abba, listened between dreams.

" 'Twas in this very spot we gathered on the night of which I will tell you. My father, the head shepherd, and very learned in the Psalms and Prophets, sat silent while the others talked softly of the flocks and of the weather, which was uncommon mild for the time of year, and of the pilgrims who had gathered out of all the provinces to pay tribute to the heathen emperor. The heavens were dark save for the great star which shamed all the rest into twinkling sparks. The young moon hung low in the west. I saw all this from the shelter of my father's cloak, and was content even as the lambs which lay close to the warm hearts of their mothers in the soft, damp grass.

"Suddenly my father lifted up his great voice. 'The Lord is in His holy temple; let all the earth keep silent before Him!' So spake he, and the others, marveling, held their peace. My young eyes were just closing in a dream of peace, but they opened wide at sound of my father's solemn voice: 'Behold I will send My messenger, and he shall prepare the way before Me: and the Lord, whom ye seek, shall suddenly come to His temple. Behold, He shall come, saith the Lord of hosts!'

"Then did the earth swoon and tremble—or so it seemed to my young fancy—and the light of the star on a sudden blazed forth with myriads of sparkling rays, of all colors splendid and rare, and radiance presently took shape to itself and became the figure

[35]

of a man clad in dazzling garments who stood over against the sleeping flocks. He spoke, and his voice was as the voice of Jordan when he rolleth his spring floods to the sea. Every man of the shepherds was fallen to the ground with fright; but I lay unafraid in the shelter of my father's cloak and saw and heard all.

"'Fear not,' said the shining one, 'for behold, I bring you good tidings of great joy, which shall be to all people. For unto you is born this day, in the city of David, a Savior, which is Christ the Lord. And this shall be a sign unto you: Ye shall find the Babe wrapped in swaddling clothes, lying in a manger.'

"Then were the heavens and the silent valley and the heights of Bethlehem filled with shining ones, who lifted up their voices in songs the like of which never yet fell on mortal ears. 'Glory to God in the highest, and on earth peace, good will toward men!' The anthem rose and fell in glorious waves of melody toward the star blazing in mid-heaven. The voices passed singing into the silence, and the shining forms, blent once more with the celestial rays of the star, wavered for an instant before our dazzled eyes, and were gone.

"My father was the first to recover himself from that trance of wonderment. 'Let us now go even to Bethlehem,' he said, 'and see this thing which is come to pass, which the Lord hath made known to us.'

"The shepherds girt themselves to depart, and I, creeping from the warm folds of the abba into the chill night, followed hard after them. Being low of stature — for I was no higher than yon little lad — I saw a thing which the others perceived not: the soft, damp grass was starred with snowy blossoms both far and near where the feet of the angels had trod. I lagged behind to gather of them a great handful.

"The dim light of the inn swung half-way up the rocky steep, and there we waited in the darkness, my young heart beating loud in my ears, whilst my father parleyed with the keeper of the gate. 'There was no babe within,' the porter said, and would have shut the door fast in our faces but that my father, being a man of authority and insisting that it was even as he had said, presently pushed by him into the khan. And indeed there was no babe in all the place, only pilgrims lying close to the sleeping-lofts and their beasts which crowded the courtyards.

"I pulled my father's sleeve and whispered to him that the angel said we should find the Babe lying in a manger. And in truth, my children, when presently we were come to the place where the great oxen were housed from the winter's cold, we found the young mother and the babe wrapped in swaddling clothes lying in a manger. He, the Salvation of Israel—the Messiah—the Desire of Nations! These eyes gazed upon Him in His beauty. These hands touched Him as He lay asleep in the manger nestled in His soft garments on the yellow straw."

The tremulous voice faltered — ceased. The old man bent forward smiling, as if once again he gazed upon the world's Savior asleep in His manger cradle.

One of the girls laid a timid finger on the border of the pilgrim's cloak. "And was He — like other babies?" she asked in a low voice.

"Like other babies?" smiled the old man. "Yea, verily, little one, He was fashioned in all points even as we are, thanks be unto Jehovah! Yet was He unlike, so wondrous fair, so heavenly beautiful was that Babe of Bethlehem as He lay even as an angel asleep in that humblest bed of all the earth. The milk-white blossoms I had gathered shone faint in the half darkness like tiny stars. I laid them at His feet and their fragrance filled all the place as incense."

[37]

The aged shepherd looked down at the flowers in his withered hands, his slow tears falling upon them like holy dew. Also he murmured strange words to which the children listened with wonder, albeit they understood them not at all. "Behold He was in the World, and the World knew him not. For by Him were all things visible and invisible, whether they be thrones, or dominions, or principalities, or powers. These things saith the Amen, the faithful and true witness."

Then the children stole quietly away one by one, till presently they were again at play amid the myriad blossoms of the star flower. But the old man rested beneath the shepherds' tower, while the shadows lengthened across the Field of Angels.

THE INN THAT MISSED ITS CHANCE

Amos R. Wells

"The Landlord Speaks: A.D. 28"

WHAT could be done, the inn was full of folks!
His honour, Marcus Lucius, and his scribes
Who made the census: honourable men
From farthest Galilee, came hitherward
To be enrolled; high ladies and their lords;
The rich, the rabbis, such a noble throng
As Bethlehem had never seen before,
And may not see again. And there they were,
Close herded with their servants, till the inn
Was like a hive at swarming-time, and I
Was fairly crazed among them.

                    Could I know
That they were so important? Just the two,
No servants, just a workman sort of man,
Leading a donkey, and his wife thereon,
Drooping and pale — I saw them not myself,
My servants must have driven them away;
But had I seen them how was I to know?
Were inns to welcome strangers, up and down
In all our towns from Beersheba to Dan,
Till he should come? And how were men to know?

There was a sign, they say, a heavenly light
Resplendent; but I had no time for stars.
And there were songs of angels in the air
Out on the hills; but how was I to hear
Amid the thousand clamours of an inn?

Of course if I had known them, who they were,
And who he that should be born that night —
For now I learn that they will make him King,
A second David, who will ransom us
From these Philistine Romans — who but he
That feeds an army with a loaf of bread,
And if a soldier falls, he touches him
And up he leaps, uninjured? Had I known,
I would have turned the whole inn upside down,
His honour, Marcus Lucius, and the rest,
And sent them all to stables, had I known.

So you have seen him, stranger, and perhaps
Again will see him. Prithee say for me,
I did not know; and if he comes again,
As he will surely come, with retinue,
And banners, and an army, tell my Lord
That all my inn is his, to make amends.

Alas! Alas! To miss a chance like that!
This inn that might be chief among them all,
The birthplace of Messiah — had I known.

"Born the King of Angels"

THE LIGHT OF BETHLEHEM

John B. Tabb

'T IS Christmas night! the snow,
　　A flock unnumbered lies;
The old Judean stars aglow,
　　Keep watch within the skies.

An icy stillness holds
　　The pulses of the night;
A deeper mystery infolds
　　The wondering Hosts of Light.

Till, lo, with reverence pale
　　That dims each diadem
The lordliest, earthward bending, hail
　　The Light of Bethlehem.

ON CHRISTMAS DAY

Elsie Williams Chandler

*D*ARKNESS had fled away,
    Starlight had led the way,
Love shone as bright as day,
        Where Jesus lay.

He was so dear and small,
    Not like a king at all,
Wrapped in His mother's shawl,
        Cradled in hay.

Stars in His mother's eyes
    Leaned down from Paradise,
Crowned God in humble guise
        Where Jesus lay.

Softly the beasts gave tongue,
    What songs they knew, they sung,
Sweetly the stable rung
        Where Jesus lay.

Lift now your voice and sing,
    Letting your carols ring
For Jesus Christ your king
        On Christmas Day.

"The Christmas Story"

WHERE IS THE BABE?

Robert Herrick

*T*ELL US, thou clear and heavenly tongue,
Where is the Babe but lately sprung,
Lies He the lily-banks among?

Or say if this new Birth of ours
Sleeps, laid within some ark of flowers,
Spangled with dew-light; thou canst clear
All doubts, and manifest the where.

Declare to us, bright star, if we shall seek
Him in the morning's blushing cheek,
Or search the beds of spices through,
To find him out?

THE FRIENDLY BEASTS

A Twelfth Century Carol

JESUS our brother, strong and good,
  Was humbly born in a stable rude,
And the friendly beasts around Him stood,
Jesus our brother, strong and good.

"I," said the donkey, shaggy and brown,
"I carried His Mother up hill and down,
"I carried her safely to Bethlehem town;
"I," said the donkey, shaggy and brown.

"I," said the cow, all white and red,
"I gave Him my manger for His bed."
"I," said the sheep with curly horn,
"I gave Him my wool for His blanket warm."

And every beast, by some good spell,
In the stable dark was glad to tell,
Of the gift he gave Immanuel,
The gift he gave Immanuel.

"Mary's Little Baby Cradled in a Stall"

VOICES IN THE MIST

Alfred, Lord Tennyson

THE time draws near the birth of Christ:
    The moon is hid; the night is still;
    The Christmas bells from hill to hill
Answer each other in the mist.

Four voices of four hamlets round,
    From far and near, on mead and moor,
    Swell out and fail, as if a door
Were shut between me and the sound:

Each voice four changes on the wind,
    That now dilate, and now decrease,
    Peace and goodwill, goodwill and peace,
Peace and goodwill, to all mankind.

THE FIRST SUPPER

Jan Struther

*A*T the First Supper
 The guests were but one:
A maiden was the hostess,
 The guest her son.

At the First Supper
 No candles were lit:
In the darkness hay-scented
 They both did sit.

At the First Supper
 No table was spread:
In the curve of her elbow
 She laid his head.

At the First Supper
 They poured no wine:
On milk of the rarest
 The guest did dine.

She held him very closely
 Against her breast,
Her fair one, her dear one,
 Her darling guest;

She held him very closely,
 Guessing that this
Is the last that any mother
 May know of bliss.

"Jesus Christ, Her Little Child"

NO ROOM AT THE INN

Author Unknown

*Y*ET if his majesty, our sovran lord,
   Should of his own accord
Friendly himself invite,
And say, "I'll be your guest tomorrow night,"
How we should stir ourselves, call and command
All hands to work! "Let no man idle stand:
Set me fine Spanish tables in the hall,
   See they be fitted all;
Let there be room to eat,
And order taken that there want no meat.
See every sconce and candlestick made bright,
That without tapers they may give a light.
Look to the presence: are the carpets spread,
   The dais o'er the head,
The cushions in the chairs,
And all the candles lighted on the stairs?
Perfume the chambers, and in any case
Let each man give attendance in his place."
Thus, if the king were coming, would we do,
   And 'twere good reason too;
For 'tis a duteous thing
To show all honour to an earthly king,
And after all our travail and our cost,
So he be pleased to think no labour lost.

But, at the coming of the King of heaven,
All's set at six and seven:
We wallow in our sin,
Christ cannot find a chamber in the inn.
We entertain him always like a stranger,
And, as at first, still lodge him in the manger.

CHILD JESUS

Hans Christian Andersen

WHEN the Christ-Child to this world came down,
He left for us His throne and crown,
He lay in a manger, all pure and fair,
Of straw and hay His bed so bare.
But high in heaven the star shone bright,
And the oxen watched by the Babe that night.
Hallelujah! Child Jesus!

Oh, come, ye sinful and ye who mourn,
Forgetting all your sin and sadness,
In the city of David a Child is born,
Who doth bring us heav'nly gladness.
Then let us to the manger go,
To seek the Christ who hath loved us so.
Hallelujah! Child Jesus!

CHRISTMAS MUSIC

Author Unknown

WHILE Mary sleeps the angels play
    A heavenly lullaby to soothe his infant sleep,
Singing their hymn of praise at close of day,
    While Joseph at the door his watch doth keep.

So, Father, at this Christmas may thy care
    Above the cradle of our little children ward;
Accepting, Lord, their infant thoughts as prayer,
    Bringing them daily nearer to their God.

"*Christmas Music*"

IN THAT SAME COUNTRY
C. F. B.

ALL the winds were dreary, dreary,
 On Judea's mountain flank—
All the trees were weary, weary,
 As their branches tossed and sank.

Winter day was dying, dying,
 In a gray-and-golden light—
Winter clouds were flying, flying,
 Out across the night.

A little maid
At the hostel door
Looked at the angry night,
And wondered why,
In the cloud-strewn sky,
One star was very bright.
The little maid
Looked down the road
And watched them climb its crest,
The woman, on the donkey's back
—Her face so white against the wrack—
Clutch at her robe of red and black.

The little maid
Could hear her lord
Shout at the bearded man
In the windy gloom:
"There is no room
Tonight in Bethl'hem khan."
The little maid
Unlatched the door
And snatched a hallway light:
"Oh, master, we can fix a bed
In the cave behind the inn," she said.
"By the manger where the calves are fed—
The lady can't ride on tonight."

All the night was leaping, leaping,
    Over old Judea's hills—
All the sheep were sleeping, sleeping,
    By the slowly purling rills.

All the stars were swinging, swinging,
    In the purple of the night—
Angels gathered, singing, singing,
    Then there was the Light.

"The Nativity"

A Prayer

OF
Saint Francis
OF Assisi

Lord make me a channel of Thy
peace
That where there is hatred —
I may bring love,
That where there is wrong — I may
bring the spirit of forgiveness,
That where there is discord — I may
bring harmony,
That where there is error — I may
bring truth,
That where there is doubt — I may
bring faith,
That where there is despair — I
may bring hope,
That where there are shadows —

I may bring Thy light,
That where there is sadness — I
may bring joy.

Lord, grant that I may seek rather
To comfort — than to be comforted;
To understand — than to be under.
stood;
To love — than to be loved;

For
It is by giving — that one receives;
It is by self-forgetting — that one
finds;
It is by forgiving — that one is forgiven;
It is by dying — that one awakens to
eternal life.

A CHRISTMAS LETTER

By Bishop Remington

I am wishing for you this Day, a happy Christmas, I would send you those gifts which are beyond price, outlast time, and bridge all space. I wish you All laughter and pure joy, a merrie heart and a clear conscience, and Love which thinks no evil, is not easily provoked, and seeks not its own. ● ● ● The fragrance of flowers, the sweet associations of holly and mistletoe and fir, the memory of deep woods,

of peaceful hills, and of the
mantling snow, which guards
the sleep of all God's
creatures. I wish that the
Spirit of Christmastide
may draw you into
companionship with Him
Who giveth all.
The little Christ-hands are
beckoning us to come within
the circle of His faith and
love, where are bright angels
and everyday saints, and all
goodness, truth and beauty.
I t is The Feast of the Child.
Come, let us adore Him."

Allah's Prayer

I pray the prayer the Easterns do. May the Peace of Allah abide with you. Wherever you stay, wherever you go, May the beautiful palms of Allah grow. Through days of labor and nights of rest, May the Love of Allah make you blest. So I touch my heart as the Easterns do. May the Peace of Allah abide with you---

DR. WATTS' CRADLE HYMN

HUSH my dear, lie still and slumber,
 holy angels guard thy bed,
Heavenly blessings without number,
 gently falling on thy head.
Sleep my babe, thy food and raiment,
 house and home thy friends provide,
All without thy care or payment,
 all thy wants are well supply'd.
How much better thou'rt attended,
 than the Son of God could be,
When from heaven he descended,
 and became a child like thee.
Soft and easy is thy cradle,
 coarse and hard thy Saviour lay,
When his birth-place was a stable,
 and his softest bed was hay.
Blessed Babe! what glorious features,
 spotless, fair divinely bright!
Must he dwell with brutal creatures,
 how could angels bear the sight!
Was there nothing but a manger,
 curséd sinners could afford,
To receive the heavenly stranger;
 did they thus affront their Lord.
Soft my child, I did not chide thee,
 tho' my song may sound too hard;
'Tis thy mother sits beside thee,
 and her arms shall be thy guard.

Yet to read the shameful story,
　　how the Jews abus'd their King,
How they serv'd the Lord of glory,
　　makes me angry while I sing.
See the kinder shepherds round him,
　　telling wonders from the sky;
There they sought him, there they found him,
　　with his Virgin Mother by.
See the Lovely Babe a-dressing;
　　lovely infant how he smil'd!
When he wept, the Mother's blessing
　　sooth'd and hush'd the holy child.
Lo! he slumbers in his manger,
　　where the hornéd oxen fed;
Peace my darling here's no danger,
　　here's no Ox a near thy bed.
'Twas to save thee, child from dying
　　save my dear from burning flame,
Bitter groans and endless crying,
　　that thy blest Redeemer came.
May'st thou live to know and fear him,
　　trust and love him all thy days!
Then go dwell for ever near him,
　　see his face and sing his praise.
I could give thee thousand kisses,
　　hoping what I most desire:
Not a mother's fondest wishes,
　　can to greater joys aspire.

From *The New England Primer*, printed in Boston, 1777

"Little Hands Outstretched to Bless"

ROBIN REDBREAST

Selma Lagerlöf

I T happened at the time when our Lord created the world, when
He not only made heaven and earth, but all the animals and the
plants as well, at the same time giving them their names.

There have been many histories concerning that time, and if
we knew them all, we should have light upon everything in this
world which we can not now comprehend.

At that time it happened one day when our Lord sat in His
Paradise and painted the little birds, that the colors in our Lord's
paint pot gave out, and the goldfinch would have been without color
if our Lord had not wiped all His paint brushes on its feathers.

It was then that the donkey got his long ears, because he could
not remember the name that had been given him.

No sooner had he taken a few steps over the meadows of Paradise than he forgot, and three times he came back to ask his name.
At last our Lord grew somewhat impatient, took him by his two
ears, and said:

"Thy name is ass, ass, ass!" And while He thus spake our
Lord pulled both of his ears that the ass might hear better, and remember what was said to him. It was on the same day, also, that
the bee was punished.

Now, when the bee was created, she began immediately to
gather honey, and the animals and human beings who caught the
delicious odor of the honey came and wanted to taste of it. But the
bee wanted to keep it all for herself and with her poisonous sting

pursued every living creature that approached her hive. Our Lord saw this, and at once called the bee to Him and punished her.

"I gave thee the gift of gathering honey, which is the sweetest thing in all creation," said our Lord, "but I did not give thee the right to be cruel to thy neighbor. Remember well that every time thou stingest any creature who desires to taste of thy honey, thou shalt surely die!"

Ah, yes! It was at that time, too, that the cricket became blind and the ant missed her wings, so many strange things happened on that day!

Our Lord sat there, big and gentle, and planned and created all day long, and towards evening He conceived the idea of making a little gray bird. "Remember your name is Robin Redbreast," said our Lord to the bird, as soon as it was finished. Then He held it in the palm of His open hand and let it fly.

After the bird had been testing his wings a while, and had seen something of the beautiful world in which he was destined to live, he became curious to see what he himself was like. He noticed that he was entirely gray, and that his breast was just as gray as all the rest of him. Robin Redbreast twisted and turned in all directions as he viewed himself in the mirror of a clear lake, but he couldn't find a single red feather. Then he flew back to our Lord.

Our Lord sat there on His throne, big and gentle. Out of His hands came butterflies that fluttered about His head; doves cooed on His shoulders; and out of the earth beneath Him grew the rose, the lily, and the daisy.

The little bird's heart beat heavily with fright, but with easy curves he flew nearer and nearer our Lord, till at last he rested on our Lord's hand. Then our Lord asked what the little bird wanted. "I only wish to ask you about one thing," said the little bird. "What is it you wish to know?" said our Lord. "Why should I be called Red Breast, when I am all gray, from the bill to the very end of my tail? Why am I called Red Breast when I do not possess one single red feather?" The bird looked beseechingly on our Lord with his tiny black eyes—then turned his head. About him he saw pheasants all red under a sprinkle of gold dust, parrots with marvelous red neckbands, cocks with red combs, to say nothing about the butterflies, the goldfinches, and the roses! And naturally he thought how little he needed—just one tiny drop of color on his breast and he, too, would be a beautiful bird, and his name would fit him. "Why should I be called Red Breast when I am so entirely gray?" asked the bird once again, and waited for our Lord to say: "Ah, my friend, I see that I have forgotten to paint your breast feathers red, but wait a moment and it shall be done."

But our Lord only smiled a little and said: "I have called you Robin Redbreast, and Robin Redbreast shall your name be, but you must look to it that you yourself earn your red breast feathers." Then our Lord lifted His hand and let the bird fly once more—out into the world.

The bird flew down into Paradise, meditating deeply.

What could a little bird like him do to earn for himself red feathers? The only thing he could think of was to make his nest in a brier bush. He built it in among the thorns in the close thicket. It looked as if he waited for a rose leaf to cling to his throat and give him color.

*   *   *   *

Countless years had come and gone since that day, which was the happiest in all the world! Human beings had already advanced so far that they had learned to cultivate the earth and sail the seas. They had procured clothes and ornaments for themselves, and had long since learned to build big temples and great cities — such as Thebes, Rome, and Jerusalem.

*   *   *   *

Then there dawned a **new** day, one that will long be remembered in the world's history. On the morning of this day Robin Redbreast sat upon a little naked hillock outside of Jerusalem's walls, and sang to his young ones, who rested in a tiny nest in a brier bush.

Robin Redbreast told the little ones all about that wonderful day of creation, and how the Lord had given names to everything, just as each Redbreast had told it ever since the first Redbreast had heard God's word, and gone out of God's hand. "And mark you," he ended sorrowfully, "so many years have gone, so many roses have bloomed, so many little birds have come out of their eggs since Creation Day, but Robin Redbreast is still a little gray bird. He has not yet succeeded in gaining his red feathers."

The little young ones opened wide their tiny bills, and asked if their forbears had never tried to do any great thing to earn the priceless red color.

"We have all done what we could," said the little bird, "but we have all gone amiss. Even the first Robin Redbreast met one day another bird exactly like himself, and he began immediately to love it with such a mighty love that he could feel his breast burn. 'Ah!' he thought then, 'now I understand! It was our Lord's meaning that I should love with so much ardor that my breast should grow red in color from the very warmth of the love that lives in my heart.' But he missed it, as all those who came after him have missed it, and as even you shall miss it."

The little young ones twittered, utterly bewildered, and already began to mourn because the red color would not come to beautify their little, downy gray breasts.

"Robin Redbreast"

"We had also hoped that song would help us," said the grown-up bird, speaking in long-drawn-out tones — "the first Robin Redbreast sang until his heart swelled within him, he was so carried away, and he dared to hope anew. 'Ah!' he thought, 'it is the glow of the song which lives in my soul that will color my breast feathers red.' But he missed it, as all the others have missed it and as even you shall miss it." Again was heard a sad "peep" from the young ones' half-naked throats.

"We had also counted on our courage and our valor," said the bird. "The first Robin Redbreast fought bravely with other birds, until his breast flamed with the pride of conquest. 'Ah!' he thought, 'my breast feathers shall become red from the love of battle which burns in my heart.' He, too, missed it, as all those who came after him have missed it, and as even you shall miss it." The little young ones peeped courageously that they still wished to try and win the much-sought-for prize, but the bird answered them sorrowfully that it would be impossible. What could they do when so many splendid ancestors had missed the mark? What could they do more than love, sing, and fight? What could — the little bird stopped short, for out of one of the gates of Jerusalem came a crowd of people marching, and the whole procession rushed toward the hillock, where the bird had its nest. There were riders on proud horses, soldiers with long spears, executioners with nails and hammers. There were judges and priests in the procession, weeping women, and above all a mob of mad, loose people running about — a filthy, howling mob of loiterers.

The little gray bird sat trembling on the edge of his nest. He feared each instant that the little brier bush would be trampled down and his young ones killed!

"Be careful!" he cried to the little defenseless young ones, "creep together and remain quiet. Here comes a horse that will ride right over us! Here comes a warrior with iron-shod sandals! Here comes the whole wild, storming mob!" Immediately the bird ceased his cry of warning and grew calm and quiet. He almost forgot the danger hovering over him. Finally he hopped down into the nest and spread his wings over the young ones.

"Oh! this is too terrible," said he. "I don't wish you to witness this awful sight! There are three miscreants who are going to be crucified!" And he spread his wings so that the little ones could see nothing.

They caught only the sound of hammers, the cries of anguish, and the wild shrieks of the mob.

Robin Redbreast followed the whole spectacle with his eyes, which grew big with terror. He could not take his glance from the three unfortunates.

"How terrible human beings are!" said the bird after a little while. "It isn't enough that they nail these poor creatures to a cross, but they must needs place a crown of piercing thorns upon the head of one of them. I see that the thorns have wounded his brow so that the blood flows," he continued. "And this man is so beautiful, and looks about him with such mild glances that every one ought to love him. I feel as if an arrow were shooting through my heart, when I see him suffer!"

The little bird began to feel a stronger and stronger pity for the thorn-crowned sufferer. "Oh! if I were only my brother the eagle," thought he, "I would draw the nails from his hands, and with my strong claws I would drive away all those who torture him!" He saw how the blood trickled down from the brow of the Crucified One, and he could no longer remain quiet in his nest. "Even if I am little and weak, I can still do something for this poor tortured one," thought the bird. Then he left his nest and flew out into the air, striking wide circles around the Crucified One. He flew around him several times without daring to approach, for he was a shy little bird, who had never dared to go near a human being. But little by little he gained courage, flew close to him, and drew with his little bill a thorn that had become imbedded in the brow of the Crucified One. And as he did this there fell on his breast a drop of blood from the face of the Crucified One; — it spread quickly and floated out and colored all the little fine breast feathers.

Then the Crucified One opened his lips and whispered to the bird: "Because of thy compassion, thou hast won all that thy kind have been striving after, ever since the world was created."

As soon as the bird had returned to his nest, his young ones cried to him: "Thy breast is red! Thy breast feathers are redder than the roses!"

"It is only a drop of blood from the poor man's forehead," said the bird; "it will vanish as soon as I bathe in a pool or a clear well."

But no matter how much the little bird bathed, the red color did not vanish — and when his little young ones grew up, the blood-red color shone also on their breast feathers, just as it shines on every Robin Redbreast's throat and breast until this very day.

THE NATIVITY

Henry Vaughan

> *T*HOU cam'st from Heaven to earth, that we
> . . . Might go from earth to Heaven with Thee:
> And though Thou found'st no welcome here,
> Thou did'st provide us mansions there—
> A stable was Thy court, and when
> Men turn'd to beasts, beasts would be men:
> They were Thy courtiers; others none;
> And their poor manger was Thy Throne;
> No swaddling silks Thy limbs did fold,
> Though Thou could'st turn Thy rags to gold.
> No rockers waited on Thy birth,
> No cradles stirred, no songs of mirth;
> But her chaste lap and sacred breast,
> Which lodged Thee first, did give Thee rest.
> But stay, what light is that doth stream
> And drop here in a gilded beam,
> It is Thy star runs page, and brings
> Thy tributary Eastern Kings.
> Lord! grant some light to us; that we
> May with them find the way to Thee!
> Behold what mists eclipse the day!
> How dark it is! Shed down one ray,
> To guide us out of this sad night,
> And say once more,
> "LET THERE BE LIGHT!"

"Christ-mas, the Light of Winter-time"

THE LITTLE GRAY LAMB

Archibald Beresford Sullivan

OUT on the endless purple hills, deep in the clasp of somber night,
　The shepherds guarded their weary ones — guarded their
flocks of cloudy white,
　　That like a snowdrift in silence lay,
　　Save one little lamb with its fleece of gray.

Out on the hillside all alone, gazing afar with sleepless eyes,
The little gray lamb prayed soft and low, its weary face to the
starry skies:
　　"O moon of the heavens so fair, so bright,
　　Give me — oh, give me — a fleece of white!"

No answer came from the dome of blue, nor comfort lurked in the
cypress-trees;
But faint came a whisper borne along on the scented wings of the
passing breeze:
　　"Little gray lamb that prays this night,
　　I cannot give thee a fleece of white."

Then the little gray lamb of the sleepless eyes prayed to the clouds
for a coat of snow,
Asked of the roses, besought the woods; but each gave answer
sad and low:
　　"Little gray lamb that prays this night,
　　We cannot give thee a fleece of white."

Like a gem unlocked from a casket dark, like an ocean pearl from its
    bed of blue,
Came, softly stealing the clouds between, a wonderful star
    which brighter grew
        Until it flamed like the sun by day
        Over the place where Jesus lay.

Ere hushed were the angels' notes of praise, the joyful shepherds
    had quickly sped
Past rock and shadow, adown the hill, to kneel at the Saviour's
    lowly bed:
        While, like the spirits of phantom night,
        Followed their flocks — their flocks of white.

And patiently, longingly, out of the night, apart from the others —
    far apart —
Came limping and sorrowful, all alone, the little gray lamb of the
    weary heart,
        Murmuring, "I must bide far away:
        I am not worthy — my fleece is gray."

And the Christ Child looked upon humbled pride, at kings bent low
    on the earthen floor,
But gazed beyond at the saddened heart of the little gray lamb
    at the open door;
And he called it up to his manger low and laid his hand on its
    wrinkled face,
While the kings drew golden robes aside to give to the weary one
    a place.

And the fleece of the little gray lamb was blest:
For, lo! it was whiter than all the rest!

In many cathedrals grand and dim, whose windows glimmer with
    pane and lens,
Mid the odor of incense raised in prayer, hallowed about
    with last amens,
The infant Saviour is pictured fair, with kneeling Magi wise and old,
But his baby-hand rests — not on the gifts, the myrrh, the
    frankincense, the gold —
      But on the head, with a heavenly light,
      Of the little gray lamb that was changed to white.

CHRISTMAS

Frank H. Sweet

HO! HO! thrice ho! for the mistletoe,
    Ho! for the Christmas holly;
And ho! for the merry boys and girls
    Who make the day so jolly.
And ho! for the deep, new-fallen snow,
    For the lace-work on each tree,
And ho! for the joyous Christmas bells
    That ring so merrily.

Ho! ho! thrice ho! for the fire's warm glow
    For the mirth and the cheer within;
And ho! for the tender, thoughtful hearts,
    And the children's merry din.
Ho! ho! for the strong and loving girls,
    For the manly, tender boys,
And ho! thrice ho! for the coming home
    To share in the Christmas joys.

Sing heigh ho! unto the green holly.

"*Sing heigh ho! unto the green holly*"

A CHRISTMAS CAROL

Christina Rossetti

IN the bleak mid-winter
    Frosty wind made moan,
Earth stood hard as iron,
    Water like a stone;
Snow had fallen, snow on snow,
    Snow on snow,
In the bleak mid-winter
    Long ago.

Our God, Heaven cannot hold him
    Nor earth sustain;
Heaven and earth shall flee away
    When he comes to reign;
In the bleak mid-winter
    A stable-place sufficed
The Lord God Almighty
    Jesus Christ.

Angels and archangels
    May have gathered there,
Cherubim and seraphim
    Thronged the air;
But only His Mother
    In her maiden bliss
Worshipped the Beloved
    With a kiss.

What can I give Him,
    Poor as I am?
If I were a shepherd
    I would bring a lamb,
If I were a Wise Man
    I would do my part —
Yet what I can I give Him,
    Give my heart.

A CHILD THIS DAY IS BORN

Early English Carol

A child this day is born, a Child of high renown;
Most worthy of a sceptre, a sceptre and a crown.
Glad tidings to all men, Glad tidings sing we may,
Because the King of Kings was born on Christmas Day.

These tidings shepherds heard, whilst watching o'er the fold;
'Twas by an angel unto them that night revealed and told.
Glad tidings to all men, glad tidings sing we may,
Because the King of Kings was born on Christmas Day.

Then was there with the angel an host incontinent,
Of heavenly bright soldiers, all from the highest sent.
Glad tidings to all men, glad tidings sing we may,
Because the King of Kings was born on Christmas Day.

They praised the Lord our God, and our Celestial King:
"All glory be in Paradise," this heavenly host did sing.
Glad tidings to all men, glad tidings sing we may,
Because the King of Kings was born on Christmas Day.

"All glory be to God, that sitteth still on high,
With praises and with triumph great, and joyful melody."
Glad tidings to all men, glad tidings sing we may,
Because the King of Kings was born on Christmas Day.

THE MINSTRELS

William Wordsworth

*T*HE minstrels played their Christmas tune
　To-night beneath my cottage-eaves;
While, smitten by a lofty moon,
　　The encircling laurels, thick with leaves,
Gave back a rich and dazzling sheen,
That overpowered their natural green.

Through hill and valley every breeze
　　Had sunk to rest with folded wings:
Keen was the air, but could not freeze,
　　Nor check, the music of the strings;
So stout and hardy were the band
That scraped the chords with strenuous hand.

And who but listened,—till was paid
　　Respect to every inmate's claim,
The greeting given, the music played
　　In honour of each household name,
Duly pronounced with lusty call,
And "Merry Christmas" wished to all.

"The Carollers"

THE CARAVAN

Ruth Sawyer

IT was winter — and twelve months since the gipsies had driven
their flocks of mountain-sheep over the dark, gloomy Balkans,
and had settled in the southlands near to the Aegean. It was twelve
months since they had seen a wonderful star appear in the sky and
heard the singing of angelic voices afar off.

They had marveled much concerning the star until a runner
had passed them from the south bringing them news that the star
had marked the birth of a Child whom the wise men had hailed as
"King of Israel" and "Prince of Peace." This had made Herod of
Judea both afraid and angry and he had sent soldiers secretly to
kill the Child; but in the night they had miraculously disappeared —
the Child with Mary and Joseph — and no one knew whither they
had gone. Therefore Herod had sent runners all over the lands that
bordered the Mediterranean with a message forbidding every one
giving food or shelter or warmth to the Child, under penalty of
death. For Herod's anger was far-reaching and where his anger fell
there fell his sword likewise. Having given his warning, the runner
passed on, leaving the gipsies to marvel much over the tale they had
heard and the meaning of the star.

Now on that day that marked the end of the twelve months
since the star had shone the gipsies said among themselves: "Dost
thou think that the star will shine again to-night? If it were true,
what the runner said, that when it shone twelve months ago it
marked the place where the Child lay it may even mark His hiding-
place this night. Then Herod would know where to find Him, and
send his soldiers again to slay Him. That would be a cruel thing
to happen!"

The air was chill with the winter frost, even there in the south-land, close to the Aegean; and the gipsies built high their fire and hung their kettle full of millet, fish, and bitter herbs for their supper. The king lay on his couch of tiger-skins, and on his arms were amulets of heavy gold, while rings of gold were on his fingers and in his ears. His tunic was of heavy silk covered with a leopard cloak, and on his feet were shoes of goat-skin trimmed with fur. Now, as they feasted around the fire a voice came to them through the darkness, calling. It was a man's voice, climbing the mountains from the south.

"Ohe! Ohe!" he shouted. And then nearer, "O-he!"

The gipsies were still disputing among themselves whence the voice came when there walked in the circle about the fire a tall, shaggy man, grizzled with age, and a sweet-faced young mother carrying a child.

"We are outcasts," said the man, hoarsely, "Ye must know that whosoever succors us will bring Herod's vengeance like a sword about his head. For a year we have wandered homeless and cursed over the world. Only the wild creatures have not feared to share their food and give us shelter in their lairs. But to-night we can go no farther; and we beg the warmth of your fire and food enough to stay us until the morrow."

The king looked at them long before he made reply. He saw the weariness in their eyes and the famine in their cheeks; he saw, as well, the holy light that hung about the child, and he said at last to his men:

"It is the Child of Bethlehem, the one they call the 'Prince of Peace.' As yon man says, who shelters them shelters the wrath of Herod as well. Shall we let them tarry?"

One of their number sprang to his feet, crying: "It is a sin to turn strangers from the fire, a greater sin if they be poor and friendless. And what is a king's wrath to us? I say bid them welcome. What say the rest?"

And with one accord the gipsies shouted, "Yea, let them tarry!"

They brought fresh skins and threw them down beside the fire for the man and woman to rest on. They brought them food and wine, and goat's milk for the Child; and when they had seen all was made comfortable for them they gathered round the Child — these black gipsy men — to touch His small white hands and feel His golden hair. They brought Him a chain of gold to play with and another for His neck and tiny arm.

"See, these shall be Thy gifts, little one," said they, "the gifts for Thy first birthday."

And long after all had fallen asleep the Child lay on His bed of skins beside the blazing fire and watched the light dance on the beads of gold. He laughed and clapped His hands together to see the pretty sight they made; and then a bird called out of the thicket close by.

"Little Child of Bethlehem," it called, "I, too, have a birth gift for Thee. I will sing Thy cradle song this night." And softly, like the tinkling of a silver bell and like clear water running over mossy places, the nightingale sang and sang, filling the air with melodies.

And then another voice called to him:

"Little Child of Bethlehem, I am only a tree with boughs all bare, for the winter has stolen my green cloak, but I also can give Thee a birth gift. I can give Thee shelter from the biting north wind that blows." And the tree bent low its branches and twined a rooftree and a wall about the Child.

Soon the Child was fast asleep, and while He slept a small brown bird hopped out of the thicket. Cocking his little head, he said:

"What can I be giving the Child of Bethlehem? I could fetch Him a fat worm to eat or catch Him the beetle that crawls on yonder bush, but He would not like that! And I could tell Him a story of the lands of the north, but He is asleep and would not hear." And the brown bird shook its head quite sorrowfully. Then it saw that the wind was bringing the sparks from the fire nearer and nearer to the sleeping Child.

"I know what I can do," said the bird joyously. "I can catch the hot sparks on my breast, for if one should fall upon the Child it would burn Him grievously."

So the small brown bird spread wide his wings and caught the sparks on his own brown breast. So many fell that the feathers were burned; and burned was the flesh beneath until the breast was no longer brown, but red.

Next morning, when the gipsies awoke, they found Mary and Joseph and the Child gone. For Herod had died, and an angel had come in the night and carried them back to the land of Judea. But the good God blessed those who had cared that night for the Child.

To the nightingale He said: "Your song shall be the sweetest in all the world, for ever and ever; and only you shall sing the long night through."

To the tree He said: "Little fir-tree, never more shall your branches be bare. Winter and summer you and your seedlings shall stay green, ever green."

Last of all He blessed the brown bird: "Faithful little watcher, from this night forth you and your children shall have red breasts, that the world may never forget your gift to the Child of Bethlehem."

A CHRISTMAS PRAYER

Charles Kingsley

OH, blessed day, which givst the eternal lie
To self and sense, and all the brute within;
Oh, come to us, amid this war of life;
    To hall and hovel come: to all who toil,
In senate, shop or study; and to those
    Who sundered by the wastes of half a world,
Ill-warned, and sorely tempted, ever face
    Nature's brute powers, and men unmanned to brutes.
Come to them, blest and blessing, Christmas Day.
    Tell them once more the tale of Bethlehem;
The kneeling shepherds, and the Babe Divine:
    And keep them men indeed, fair Christmas Day.

"Light of Light"

CHRISTMAS MORNING

Elizabeth Madox Roberts

IF Bethlehem were here today
Or this were very long ago,
There wouldn't be a winter time
Nor any cold or snow.

I'd run out through the garden gates,
And down along the pasture walk;
And off beside the cattle barns
I'd hear a kind of gentle talk.

I'd move the heavy iron chain
And pull away the wooden pin:
I'd push the door a little bit
And tiptoe very softly in.

The pigeons and the yellow hens
And all the cows would stand away;
Their eyes would open wide to see
A lady in the manger hay,
If this were very long ago
And Bethlehem were here today.

And Mother held my hand and smiled —
I mean the lady would — and she
Would take the woolly blankets off
Her little boy so I could see.

His shut-up eyes would be asleep,
And he would look just like our John,
And he would be all crumpled too,
And have a pinkish color on.

I'd watch his breath go in and out,
His little clothes would be all white,
I'd slip my finger in his hand
To feel how he could hold it tight.

And she would smile and say, "Take care,"
The Mother, Mary, would, "Take care";
And I would kiss his little hand
And touch his hair.

While Mary put the blankets back
The gentle talk would soon begin,
And when I'd tiptoe softly out
I'd meet the wise men going in.

"Yea, Lord We Greet Thee"

LO, IN THE SILENT NIGHT

Fifteenth Century Poem

*L*O, in the silent night a child to God is born,
    And all is brought again that ere was lost or lorn.
Could but thy soul, O man, become a silent night,
God would be born in thee, and set all things aright."

GOD BLESS THE LITTLE THINGS

Margaret Murray

*G*OD bless the little things this Christmastide,
　All the little wild things that live outside;
Little cold robins and rabbits in the snow,
Give them good faring and a warm place to go;
All little young things for His sake Who died,
Who was a Little Thing at Christmastide.

"The Birds' Breakfast"

THE VIRGIN MARY TO THE CHILD JESUS

Elizabeth Barrett Browning

SLEEP, sleep, mine Holy One,
  My flesh, my Lord — what name?
    I do not know
A name that seemeth not too high, too low
  Too far from me, or heaven:
My Jesus, that is best — that word being given
By the majestic angel, whose command
Was softly, as a man's beseeching, said,
When I and all the earth appeared to stand
    In the great overflow
Of light celestial from his wings and head.
    Sleep, sleep, my saving One.

And art thou come for saving, baby-browed
And speechless Being — art thou come for saving?
The palm that grows beside our door is bowed
By treading of the low wind from the south,
A restless shadow through the chamber waving:
Upon its bough a bird sings in the sun;
But thou, with that close slumber on thy mouth,
Dost seem of wind and sun already weary.
Art thou come for saving, O my Weary One?
Perchance this sleep, that shutteth out the dreary
Earth-sounds and motions, opens on thy soul

High dream's on fire with God;
High songs that make the pathways where they roll
More bright than stars do theirs; and visions new
Of thine Eternal Nature's old abode.
       Suffer this Mother's kiss,
       Best thing that earthly is,
To glide the music and the glory through,
Nor narrow in thy dreams the broad upliftings
       Of any seraph wing.
Thus noiseless, thus. Sleep, sleep, my Dreaming One.

The slumber of his lips meseems to run
Through my lips to mine heart, to all its shiftings
Of sensual life, bringing contrariousness
In a great calm. I feel I could lie down,
As Moses did, and die — and then live most.
I am 'ware of you, heavenly presences,
That stand with your peculiar light unlost,
Each forehead with a high thought for a crown,
Unsunned in the sunshine. I am 'ware. Ye throw
No shade against the wall. How motionless
Ye round me with your living statuary,

While, through your whiteness, in and outwardly,
Continual thoughts of God appear to go,
Like light's soul in itself. I bear, I bear
To look upon the dropped lids of your eyes,
Though their external shining testifies
To that beatitude within which were
Enough to blast an eagle at his sun:

I fall not on my sad clay face before ye —
    I look on his. I know
My spirit, which dilateth with the woe
      Of his mortality,
      May well contain your glory.
      Yea, drop your lids more low.
Ye are but fellow-worshippers with me.
    Sleep, sleep, my Worshipped One.

We sate among the stalls at Bethlehem;
The dumb kine from their fodder turning them,
    Softened their hornéd faces
      To almost human gazes
      Towards the newly born:
The simple shepherds from the star-lit brooks
      Brought visionary looks,
As yet, in their astonied hearing, rung
    The strange sweet angel-tongue:
The Magi of the east, in sandals worn,
    Knelt reverent, sweeping round,
With long pale beards, their gifts upon the ground
    The incense, myrrh and gold
These baby hands were impotent to hold:
So, let all earthlies and celestials wait
    Upon thy royal state.
    Sleep, sleep, my kingly One.

I am not proud — meek angels, ye invest
New meekness to hear such utterance rest
On mortal lips — 'I am not proud' — not proud:

Albeit, in my flesh God sent his son;
Albeit, over him my head is bowed
As others bow before him; still mine heart
Bows lower than their knees.

I often wandered forth, more child than maiden,
Among the midnight hills of Galilee
    Whose summits looked heavy-laden,
Listening to silence, as it seemed to be
God's voice, so soft yet strong, so fain to press
Upon my heart, as heaven did upon the height,
And waken up its shadow by a light,
And show its vileness by a holiness.
Then I knelt down most silent like the night,
    Too self-renounced for fears,
Raising my small face to the boundless blue
Whose stars did mix and tremble in my fears
God heard them falling after with his dew.

    Ah, King; ah, Christ; ah, son;
    Sleep, sleep, my kingly One.

Art thou a King, then? Come, his universe,
    Come, crown me him a King.
Pluck rays from all such stars as never fling
    Their light where fell a curse,
And make a crowning for his kingly brow.

Unchildlike shade. No other babe doth wear
An aspect very sorrowful, as thou.

No small babe-smiles my watching heart has seen
To float like speech, the speechless lips between;
No dovelike cooing in the golden air;
No quick short joys of leaping babyhood:
    Alas, our earthly good
In heaven thought evil, seems too good for thee:
    Yet, sleep my weary One.
And then, the drear sharp tongue of prophecy,
With the dread sense of things that shall be done,
Doth smite me inly, like a sword: a sword?
That 'smites the Shepherd.' Then, I think aloud
The words 'despised,' 'rejected' — every word
Recoiling into darkness, as I view
    The Darling on my knee.
Bright angels, move not — lest ye stir the cloud
Betwixt my soul and his futurity.
I must not die, with Mother's work to do,
    And could not live — and see.

    That tear fell not on thee.
Beloved; yet, thou stirrest in thy slumber,
Thou, stirring not for glad sounds out of number
Which, through the vibratory palm trees, run
    From summer-wind and bird,
    So quickly hast thou heard
    A tear fall silently?
    Wak'st thou, O loving One?

A LULLABY FOR THE BABY JESUS

Czech Carol

*L*ITTLE JESUS, sweetly sleep, do not stir;
  We will lend a coat of fur.
We will rock you, rock you, rock you,
We will rock you, rock you, rock you:

See the fur to keep you warm,
Snugly round your tiny form.
Mary's little baby, sleep, sweetly sleep,
Sleep in comfort, slumber deep;

We will rock you, rock you, rock you,
We will rock you, rock you, rock you:
We will serve you all we can,
Darling, darling little man.

"The Crib"

CHRISTMAS ALWAYS

Cynthia Hurst

*T*HERE'LL always be a Christmas—
    The bells, the candle glow,
And babies' stockings by the fire
    Because we will it so.

There'll always be glad greetings
    To ring through every land,
And carollers will sing to hearts,
    And hearts will understand.

We'll always watch the heaven,
    Watch one star's Christmas glow—
We'll always have a Christmas,
    God help us keep this so!